PULLING WEEDS
TO PICKING STOCKS

PULLING WEEDS TO PICKING STOCKS

THE ADOLESCENT MILLIONAIRE

BY THE BEATTY BOYS

TATE PUBLISHING & Enterprises

Published by Tate Publishing & Enterprises, LLC
127 E. Trade Center Terrace | Mustang, Oklahoma 73064 USA
1.888.361.9473 | www.tatepublishing.com

Tate Publishing is committed to excellence in the publishing industry. The company reflects the philosophy established by the founders, based on Psalms 68:11,
"The Lord gave the word and great was the company of those who published it."

Book design copyright © 2008 by Tate Publishing, LLC. All rights reserved.
Cover design by Janae Glass
Interior design by Jennifer L. Fisher
Illustrations by Kathy Hoyt

Published in the United States of America

ISBN: 978-1-60462-787-9

1. Juvenile Nonfiction: Business and Economics
08.04.15

This book was written for
anyone who has a desire to succeed.

Acknowledgments

We want to say thanks to our family for the constant push and encouragement to go after our dreams. Additionally, we want to thank the people we have come across in our lives, many being positive examples and supporting what our family already encouraged.

I would like to give a special thank you to my brothers, Devin and Deric, whose ideas were an important part of this book and I am glad they were part of this process.

Thank you.

Table of Contents

Introduction

Hi, we are David, Devin, and Deric–"The Beatty Brothers."
We would like to share our story on how we became rich.

In this book we will show you the basic fundamental
foundation we used to help us along the path of success.

We would like you to know that both adults and
people younger than adults have read this book and have
given us the "thumbs up." So don't think you can't read it
because you *can*.

There are nine steps we want to share with you.

- Choice of Actions

- Yahoo! Finance

- Guilt

- Tithing 101–What is it?

- Debt–It takes a Boy Scout

- Refrigerator Job Board

- Pulling Weeds

- Emergency Preparedness

- Believe in Yourself

There are three main steps we want you to know.

- Choice of Actions

- Tithing 101

- Believe in Yourself

Okay, the moment you have all been waiting for, who are these boys and why do they think they can teach us about money?

My name is David, I am sixteen years old and worked with my brothers and became rich. I spent the first twelve years of my life building Lego cities and helping my mom do odd jobs around the house, like build fire pits and rock walkways, and of course, the dishes. I like to kayak, hike, and draw house designs and layouts. I shoot my pellet gun and have airsoft wars with my friends. I am on the high school honor roll and received my letter in swimming. I do many service-type jobs, but mostly enjoy the time we get as a family to play games like Monopoly and Risk. As I am writing this, it is 100 degrees outside and we've just come in from a water balloon fight.

Here is my brother Devin, the typist of the book.

Thanks, David. I'm Devin; I'm fourteen. I have a few heroes in my life. My dad and Scrooge are two of them. I spend most of my days writing books, playing knights with Deric, and collecting pennies. I have been trying to double my pennies every day. I have cashed a lot of my birthday money and money from jobs into pennies, and some half dollars; I keep them all loose. I am a member of the National Junior Honor Society at my middle school. My mom homeschooled me for several years off and on, same with my brothers. I play the trumpet and like to swim. I am known to be quite shy and like magic and comedy. My favorite cartoon is Calvin and Hobbs. My favorite place to hike is in Arches National Park and hidden trails along the Colorado River.

But my real interest is money; I like seeing how it works, how it's affected, and what it is good for if it is not based on anything like gold or silver.

Here is Deric.

Hi, I am Deric, and I'm almost eight. I want to find hidden treasure. I am going to be a football player in college and then be a warrior, probably a Navy Seal or a Force Recon guy. I love fishing. I collect nickels, quarters, diamonds, rocks, gold, silver, and other neat things.

(Deric doesn't really have any diamonds, just gemstones our mom puts in our treasure hunts.)

Over the years we have watched our parents talk about goals and set out to follow them. We have seen both the success and "failure." We have watched them turn these experiences into things that help them in their future choices. And when we ask about trying out our own ideas they are usually right there encouraging the way.

Devin has always wanted to write and publish a book. He has several started and even wrote a "choose your own adventure" for Deric's birthday. He'll more than likely succeed in this publishing adventure. Almost everyone we know looks forward to hearing what Devin has written in between their visits.

David, on the other hand, builds ways to capture or harness energy from wind and water. When we drive down the road, he usually has a new design he wants to test out the window. He also likes to spend time trying to come up with new ways to create power and has some intriguing ideas. It is definitely something that he is good at—well, that and designing houses. There is a piece of land with sixty-five building sites set up with water and power that David says if he had enough money he would design a housing development and has already drawn the architectural layouts for the houses. People like to see his latest work when they visit.

Deric is pretty much determined that he will be some sort of knight when he grows up and practices shooting his arrows and sword play. He loves to be read to and is an excellent bookmark maker.

When we decided to write a book together our parents naturally said, "You should see what you can do!" Obviously, this book you are about to read is what we could do. Our mom helped with some of the editing and we think the result is promising.

Our mom said that when we started to come up with ideas, we should use one that everyone could benefit from—something that we learned and could share. At first we had no idea what to write about but quickly came to the conclusion to write about money.

We hope that you can gain something from reading our story, something that you may be able to share with others along the way.

Laying the Foundation

Who are these guys?

Our story begins long before we were born in the home of our parents and probably their parents' parents, and their parents' parents' parents… To shorten that a bit we'll begin in the home of our mom.

At birth, our mom entered a traditional household with one older sister and eventually five more siblings. Her dad worked in the insurance industry and her mom kept the kids current on their activities. Money wasn't talked about directly. Her parents only spoke of money on a rare occasion in front of the kids and even at that, it was very brief. She learned what she could through the habits of her parents.

One day her father took time to talk a little bit about stocks. Her father said it was a way she could own part of a company and used Disney as an example. She became so excited that she could own part of Disneyland that she was content for quite a while.

Her grandfather owned National Indemnity Insurance and sold his company to Warren Buffet in 1967. Her family then owned, and we guess part of them still does, multiple shares of that stock.

She said she never felt rich; everyone was always included in all of their activities. Her father helped families who could otherwise not afford nice things have a chance to experience them.

Then one day their life changed and they were living in a hotel. She began to understand what was going on financially. Again through listening in on her parents' conversations, she learned the Berkshire stock (class A) had been sold, the money spent, and no real income was coming in. She saw the stress of no money, she saw her mom sad, she saw them drift apart, and the family she knew changed. She began thinking about how she could make money and ways to bring her family back together.

She let us read her diaries she kept during that time and it was interesting to learn about her thoughts when she was our age.

To sum it up she says the most important thing she learned was the value of family, not the things you have, and by having your family as something to believe in, you can help many more people.

She was also determined to do something, but it was not written down. When we ask her about it she says, "I just didn't want to quit. I didn't like losing. But I also didn't think I had any other options available in my future. Growing up was confusing for me; it didn't come easy. But I never lost hope." When we see our mom work, she really shows us what she meant about not quitting. This is true, except when it comes to cleaning the house every day. (Don't worry, Mom, not many people are going to read this, and besides, pre-wrinkled clothes take the stress out of having to iron!)

Aside from the importance of family, this is what our mom says, a lot:

"Boys, the best news I can give you is you have a brain! And you can use it! I don't say this to put you down, *you* have a lot of the help you need already inside *you!*

"Your brain runs without designer labels and exotic foods. It also can find happiness without the T.V. Amazing! You have your own personal computer, capable of reading, writing, solving basic to complex math problems, and creating ideas. It can choose between right and wrong and it knows what is best for *you*. The only thing you have to do is use it!"

Let's move on to our dad's (stepdad's) side of the story. Oh wait, one more thing about our mom—she is fun and we love her.

Okay, back to our dad.

He grew up in a little town; his parents are still married and happy together. He is smart and likes energy/science. His mom was a state representative in Iowa, and his dad has a PhD in political science. We have a lot of fun with our grandma and grandpa; we ride bikes, work in the garden, and go on family trips to places like Yellowstone and Snowmass, Colorado.

Our dad got a savings bond for $3,000 and a friend of his in college showed him about investing. So while he was in the Navy, our dad invested in mutual funds that included the S&P (Standard & Poor's) and Emerging Markets (which our parents call emergency markets). Unlike our mom's house, our dad's was calmer and more stable. He saw his uncles and aunts and grandparents all the time. His mom made him and his sister pull one hundred weeds from the yard in the summers, and he had no idea what he really wanted to do when he grew up when he was our age.

He spent many days collecting stamps and coins. He has tried to get us interested in these as well; we like them but don't like to organize them like he does.

Our dad works really hard; when he says he'll do something, he gives it more than 100%. He doesn't like to be late (Mom); he has the same breakfast every single morning: a bowl of Cheerios—sometimes mom will put sliced bananas in it and he acts like he's never had that done before and thanks her, and Mom just smiles and pats his back.

Our parents have two totally different upbringings. And that is where they learned their financial foundations, sort of.

· · ·

We figured if most people learn about money in their mid to late thirties then we have a pretty good head start. As the old saying goes, "It is up to you to make you what you are."

Accountability

What is accountability? Having the strength of your own convictions? In our house we hear this quite often. Maybe not in those same words each time, but they all mean the same: having a choice, making a choice, and living with the consequences. It also means standing up for what you believe in.

Do you believe in something? It is really important to believe in something. It could be your family, it could be not chewing gum, or it could be the way you mow your lawn.

When you believe in something you are giving yourself a goal or a standard to live up to. You aren't just floating around; you actually have something to strive for.

Ever since we were born, our parents set strict guidelines for us to follow, a standard to live up to. We knew not to ask for checkout candies. One time one of us took a pack of gummies and started sharing it when we got to the car. Mom saw this and took us back into the store, asked for the store manager, and made the three-year-old gummy snatcher give back what he had taken. That was a long time ago and we still remember it.

So how does taking a pack of gummies when you are three set a financial foundation? Throughout the years, it has served as a springboard for many conversations, like working, how many pennies it takes to buy the pack, what happens when you take something that doesn't belong to you, and the feelings that go along with that choice. It also sets up the ability to show the link our choices make—how, in a sense, we can affect others. It doesn't mean we are responsible for other people's choices, but we can affect their ability to do things.

Let us use the following example:

You have been asked to mow the yard. You weren't given a time frame to get the job done; it was just a request that your mother gave to you as she was walking by with a load of laundry.

There are three choices here. The first choice is you get up and go mow the lawn (because you know if you are asked, it usually means right away). The second is you wait until you are asked five more times, and the third is you ignore the request and continue doing what you want.

Let's see what happens in choice number one, immediate response:

There you are, immersed in your video game; your mom looks at you and says, "Could you please mow the lawn so we can put the weed getter on the grass and edge the sides?"

You then find a good place to pause the game, get your shoes on, and head out the door. You check to make sure there is gas in the tank and enough oil. You push the mower to your normal starting place, pump the primer, pull the cord, and start mowing. You mow close to the edges, catch the grass in the mulch bag, empty the grass from the mulch bag, and continue until your job is done. Then your dad puts the weed and feed out and your brother (if you have one) can weed eat along the edges. You all put your tools away and can now get ready for a dinner without a lecture on getting jobs done on time. Choice one seems simple and time effective.

Let's see what happens in choice number two, waiting until begged:

There are, immersed in your video game; your mom looks at you and says, "Could you please mow the lawn so we can put the weed getter on the grass and edge the sides?"

You continue to play your game like there was a slight breeze in your ear, but you are too focused on what you are doing to notice. Again, the question is asked, "Please mow the lawn so we can go to put the weed getter on the grass and edge the sides, and then we can have a nice dinner."

You think in your head, *La la la. I like my video game. La la la. There must be a draft in the room; it sounds like: mow the lawn.*

Now the third time is getting a little annoying; why can't anyone see you are in the middle of something important? No one has passed this level before! So, when you are told, "I need you to mow the lawn so we can get the other chores done before dark. Please say yes if you understand." You say, "Yes, I heard you; just give me a second. This is a really hard level."

Fifteen minutes later, you are at the pinnacle of your video game career and your mom says, "Turn off the game and go mow the lawn." Her tone isn't the friendliest and she is starting to have steam come out the top of her head. So you say, "*Fine*, I am turning it off." Your mom walks away and you work on finding a good place to save the game.

Thirty minutes later, your mom unplugs the TV and takes the control from your hand. You get up and start finding your shoes. Once outside you see your dad is mowing the yard when he was supposed to be getting the oil changed in the car.

Now it is getting late and you take over the mowing job and push along at a quick pace. You miss only a few spots, but enough to make the yard look like it got a cheap haircut. Your dad gets the oil changed in the car but doesn't have time to get the weed and feed out, and your brother doesn't have time to finish weed eating the edges. But at least the yard mowing got done.

This choice seemed to be a little irritating and not very time effective. And the mood isn't the best for a family game.

Now, let's see what happens in choice number three, hiding:

There you are, immersed in your video game; your mom looks at you and says, "Could you please mow the lawn so we can put the weed getter on the grass, and edge the sides?"

Pretending she was talking to your brother (who is in the kitchen washing dishes), you stop the video game, get up, and run as fast as you can to your room without being seen.

Your mom continues on her laundry mission and thinks you've gone out to do your chores. She is happy and in a good mood, glowing with pride that she has a child so willing to help.

After folding the laundry and checking on the kitchen clean up, she looks out the window to smile at you, but alas, you are not out there. Oh you must be talking with your father, what a good child you are, *smile smile*.

Your dad walks in thirty minutes later to get a drink. You hear your mom say she was just about to bring you and your dad a drink, and then you hear the words, "I haven't seen him; I thought he was in here with you."

Oh doom and gloom! You bunker down and pick up a book to read under your bed. You hear the lawn mower turn on about an hour later, that is after your name has been called a few times.

A few hours later the tools have been put away and everyone is tired and wants to rest. You come out of hiding and say, "Let's play a game or something," and everyone else says they just want to rest. Then you are all disappointed that you don't get to play; you're not tired.

Well, as you can see, and also assume, this choice wasn't the best. People were tired and cranky because they were counting on you to help, which would have allowed them to get their projects done on time as well. Instead, they had to do your work and didn't finish theirs, leaving a rollover of projects for the next day. And you didn't get the fun evening you were counting on.

You should take a minute to think about what you believe in and what kind of person you want to be. If you were asked for help or given an assignment, what choice would you pick?

How does this work with the financial base? Well it shows what kind of person you are. You like to be actively involved in your life, meaning you want to guide where your choices lead you—choice number one above.

You could wait until someone else pushes you to do something, letting someone else guide your choices by not paving your own path—choice number two above. The last option is that you want others to do the work so you don't have to. You hope to still get a good deal without putting in any effort, not guiding the direction your life is going. The results: you don't care—choice number three above. If you don't care, then you don't really believe in something, because if you did you wouldn't let yourself be blindly led by others.

Have you ever taken a leap of faith? We have one story that shows your right to choose, even if it is not the best choice. Here is the story told by our mom:

We spent a week in Moab, Utah, shopping in the local stores, eating ice cream, rafting down the Colorado River, hiking in Arches National Park, and stargazing in the clearest sky you could ever imagine.

We tried to get a long hike in each day, hoping to use some of the endless energy the boys have. While strolling along one of the numerous trails in Arches National Park, we stopped to look at an extraordinary slot canyon. Here, the steep cliffs fell upon a pool of particularly deep, soft, red sand. David and Devin lay in the sand, soaking in its unique texture as they lifted handfuls into the air and let it sneak out through their fingers.

Ted and Devin noticed a ledge that ran from a few feet above the floor to about thirty feet above the floor. With a flash of excitement in their eyes they started to climb, with David hot on their heals. Initially they began crawling along the ledge and soon rose to walk along the widening space. Once they reached the end of the road they stopped to throw out some echoes and wave to me below. Deric, who was along for the ride strapped to my back, began to get uncomfortable and I called to the boys above that it was time to come down for lunch. At some point along the path down, Devin called out asking if he could jump. Thinking he meant when he got lower to the floor I said, "Yep, when you come down a bit farther." I think he only heard the yep.

Before I could do anything and before Ted could grab him, he leaped, soaring high above my head. I watched as his little body floated almost motionless for a moment before he sped downward. Like watching a slow motion movie in high speed, he fell through the air, down, down,

down; he brushed quickly through my outreached arms and hit the velvety soft sand like a boulder hits cement. As he hit the sand, he sank in an inch or so. His legs gave way and his bottom acted as a small shock absorber for the majority of his weight. Stunned, I quickly and carefully approached his lifeless body, desperately trying to remember the part of my first aid class that covered "what to do if your child jumps off a cliff."

Ted, in the meantime, had jumped off a lower section and ran to the car for anything that might help. I touched Devin's curled shoulders just as he began to roll. He rolled over and over, and then hushed grunting noises started to come out with his breath. David stood behind me, hoping his brother would be all right. By the time Ted returned, Devin was running through the canyon once again. His back was sore, but he said he felt fine. We took him to get checked in Moab, to be on the safe side, and amazingly enough he landed without a scratch inside or out. To this day, however, we have not forgotten "Devin's giant jump."

Wow, what a jump! Thanks for telling the story.

There are many ways we can look at this situation. First we can evaluate the choice Mom made to say "yep" as the first word when talking to a six-year-old, and then the choice that Devin made standing on the ledge. It is like taking a leap of faith. When Devin jumped, all he thought of was jumping into a swimming pool. He assumed he would be safe. So he jumped.

That jump changed his life. Before it he was totally trusting and had complete faith in his safety. But then he became more and more wary. It is kind of like trust; we all have it but once it's been broken it takes a long time to restore.

So this could be compared to a test of character. You can't let the result determine the rest of your life. You have to get up and shake the dirt off. He just learned a valuable lesson: don't jump off a cliff. Devin can remember that jump and learn from it and use it for the rest of his life.

Good going, Devin! Way to learn and apply!

Yahoo! Finance

Now we are going to skip to a little money talk. We got our first portfolios soon after the "giant jump." Dad set us up with a Yahoo! Finance portfolio. We got to pick companies and we each had $1,000 of imaginary money to spend. We picked things we knew offhand. Hershey's, Pepsi; we asked if we could own part of the University of Texas, Ford Motors, and United Airlines. As you can see, we skipped all over and were pretty diverse in our thinking. Devin is our commodities guy. He tends to think along the base. Every day we would come in and ask how our stocks were doing.

What benefit did this have on a six- and eight-year-old? Not too much at the time, we thought. The stocks were like a game, something dad was reading about often. Our parents never hid the choices they were making financially, and we got a chance to see the results, whatever they were.

Even though we thought we weren't benefiting, we were actually learning a language. Some people have bilingual parents and grow up knowing two languages. Well, economics is our second. No, we are not even close to fluent in this language but we are working on it.

So our second financial layer is really education. Not the school kind, but learning to educate yourself by paying attention. What are ways you can educate yourself and how can you start investigating companies for investment?

If you don't know, pick a store you like to shop in. Visit their Web site and go to the corporate info. Or you can go to Yahoo! Finance and type in the company on the "look up ticker" link. Read about the officers, their history, and what they project for the future. Find another company, do the same thing, compare companies.

Now move on to industries. Start with what you know and see what areas affect that industry. If it is a grocery store, does the price of metal or the price of corn affect it?

Do you want to learn what renewable energy is? Find out! Start by calling the electric company and ask what it is, read the company Web site, learn about the resources (where the power comes from), who owns them, how reliable they are, and the costs.

The more you learn about something, the more you are aware where your money is going when you spend it. Let us give you another example. What is a way for you to balance the price of gasoline you pay at the pump? Try this:

Where does the gas at the pump come from?

_____

Where did that company get it?

_____

What was involved in refining it?

_____

What company brought it to the refinery?

_____

Did that company pull it from the ground?

_____

Aside from oil wells, are there other places oil can be found?

_____

_____

_____

What happens when we use our corn for cars? Well, our farm animals don't get it. The price of milk goes up, which means the price of ice cream, cheese, yogurt, soups, chocolate, bread, school lunches, restaurant foods, and many more things increase.

If prices go up then you need more money to buy these items. And if you are always working to make more money to keep up with prices, how can you get ahead?

See, that is what we mean by education. If you take time to learn these things, then you can find a way to use what you learn to make money.

These connections are rather big spider webs. Have you ever thought about what would happen if we did not use crude oil anymore? Did you ever think of the products, aside from gas and power, that might be affected?

• • •

About once every few weeks we get to hear the Rush Limbaugh radio show. There are several reasons we like to hear him. One being he believes in people. If we were to tell him we wanted to write this book, you know what he'd say? "Go for it!" Now we don't want to put words into his mouth, so maybe we will call and ask him.

The other reason we like to listen is he's made mistakes and has been lied about. Well, we've made mistakes and were expected not to quit, and he didn't quit either. He reinforces that just because you trip or people say things about you, talk behind your back, or even to your face, the only person that can bring you down is you. Things hurt your feelings, things aren't fair; we have seen people close to us get hurt by lies and they kept going. So when we listen to the show we understand why he tries to keep encouraging people to succeed, even if it's a tough environment.

In one of his programs he ended by talking about things that are made from drilling oil. He was talking about this because he was trying to show that oil is a much bigger part of our lives than most people think.

Due to it being the end of the show he had to wrap things up quickly and left a few things out. So we wanted to help him; here is a list of *some* of the things that are made from oil:

1. Books
2. Lego's
3. Bikes
4. Floor wax
5. Sports Car Bodies
6. Tires
7. Dishwashing Soaps
8. Plastic Dishes
9. Toothbrushes
10. Toothpaste
11. Combs
12. Tents
13. Hair Curlers
14. Lipstick
15. Ice Cube Trays
16. Electric Blankets
17. Tennis Rackets
18. Hoses
19. House Paint
20. Roller Blade Wheels
21. Instrument Strings
22. Organic Product Containers
23. Eyeglasses
24. Ice Chests and Coolers
25. Lifejackets
26. TV Cabinets
27. Computers
28. Insect Repellent
29. Refrigerants
30. DVDs
31. Cold Cream
32. Glycerin
33. Plywood Adhesive
34. Cameras
35. Anesthetics
36. Artificial Turf
37. Fake Plants
38. Bandages
39. Dentures
40. Mops
41. Beach Umbrellas
42. Ballpoint pens
43. Boats
44. Nail Polish
45. Golf Bags
46. Caulking

47. Tape Recorders
48. Curtains
49. Vitamin Capsules
50. Dashboards
51. Putty
52. Coffee Makers
53. Skis
54. Insecticides
55. Fishing lures
56. Perfumes
57. Shoe Polish
58. Petroleum Jelly
59. Faucet Washers
60. Food Preservatives
61. Antihistamines
62. Plastic Wrap
63. Wax Paper
64. Sandwich bags
65. Tupperware
66. Cortisone
67. Dyes
68. Kitchen Utensils
69. Hot Pads
70. Cups
71. Plates
72. Rafts
73. Solvents
74. Roofing
75. Clothing Ink
76. PVC Piping
77. Crayons
78. Parachutes
79. Telephones
80. Enamel
81. Scotch Tape
82. Antiseptics
83. Vacuum Cleaners
84. Deodorant
85. Pantyhose
86. Rubbing Alcohol
87. Carpets
88. Epoxy Paint
89. Filters
90. Upholstery
91. Hearing Aids
92. Car sound Insulation

93. Cassette Tapes
94. Helmets
95. Pillows
96. Shower Doors
97. Shoes
98. Refrigerator linings
99. Electrical tape
100. Safety glass
101. Awnings
102. Salad Bowls
103. Rubber Cement
104. Nylon Rope
105. Ice Buckets
106. Fertilizers
107. Hair Coloring
108. Toilet Seats
109. Denture Glue
110. Loudspeakers
111. Movie Film
112. Backpacking Supplies
113. Candles
114. Car Polish
115. Shower Curtains
116. Credit/Debit/Gift Cards
117. Aspirin
118. Golf Balls
119. Detergents
120. Sunglasses
121. Glue
122. Linoleum
123. Plastic Wood
124. Soft Contact Lenses
125. Trash Bags
126. Hand Lotion
127. Shampoo
128. Shaving Cream
129. Footballs
130. Paint Brushes
131. Balloons
132. Fan Belts
133. Kayaks
134. Paint Rollers
135. Luggage
136. Fake Leather

Okay so now that you've seen our pages on oil products, why is this important?

All these prices will vary, like the corn/milk example earlier. If you know this information and you know that oil is going to remain a much-needed commodity in the future, where would you put your money?

We personally put money in sand. Now you will have to research for yourself to see what we are talking about and then you can decide. Use your brain; was it a good idea?

The other thing we want you to see is nothing you do is superficial. There are always layers. Your choices are the same. Whatever you do has an effect. You may not see the effect immediately; it could be years later. That is why it is important for you to pay attention, learn what you can, and share your findings.

Habits

What does education have to do with habits?

A habit is a learned behavior that you can do without consciously thinking, an acquired behavior pattern regularly followed until it has become almost involuntary; mental character or disposition. But as we have said before, you have a brain!

We are sure at some time in your life you have heard someone say, "Use your brain." Believe us, *we have heard that a lot!* We are told to use our brains or to explain, "What in the world we were thinking."

What is a comfort zone? Taking a freezing cold shower will break you from your comfort zone for sure.

Your comfort zone is created by the desire to stay within the confines of what you know, like a safety net. The best cure for this is something just as important as thinking, and that is *learning.*

The more you learn, the more you grow; you can learn through books (like this one), you can listen to others, and the best of all, you can learn through your own experience. There are people around you all the time; watch, listen, and ask questions.

Think about the choices you've made. Did they work? What were the results? We are sure you have also heard this, "The only mistakes are the ones we did *not* learn from."

Learning enables us to become more appreciative of many things. Not to mention, the more you learn, the more you can share. By sharing, you are helping others, and by helping others, you grow and continue to contribute to your brain. This cycle never fails. The only way to break it is to stop trying, stop learning, and stop helping.

When you learn and use your brain, you become more aware, more alert, and with that, your habits can be swayed or changed into something more positive. And creating a good habit can be a family affair.

Here is a habit we've learned. One of us was very bossy. Mom said that this particular one of us learned it from his brothers. We all know that is impossible, due to the fact that the brothers were practically perfect (ha!).

So we went into an attitude boot camp. We were asked to watch our tone of voice and the words we used. And Mom was right there catching every single slip. Every negative tone, every pessimistic comment, every grab for a toy with out asking, and even with asking and then snatching, she was there clearing her throat and smiling the "I'm watching you" smile.

Then something happened. A few months later we noticed that things were a little different in our house. We had a dictatorship, just kidding. No really, we weren't arguing as much and we actually were able to help each other without looking for something in return. See, it was a family affair. And it lasted for a while!

What habits do you have? What habits have you made? What habits have you broken? One habit that is important to look at is how you spend money.

The big thing in our house is food. Mom has said that we are now responsible to make our own food if we want to eat outside of mealtime. Additionally, we are responsible for our groceries for the whole family.

Mom let us buy, the first few times, whatever we wanted. By the end of the week we were hungry. We had to find another way to use the money we were given in order for us to not starve. This means we don't get a lot of pre-made foods. The only ready-to-eat food either comes from our garden or in the form of apples and fruit and veggies. Yes, this was a habit we had to acquire. When we (Mom) have to make our food from scratch, it saves us a lot of money.

When listening to our mom talk to women about home economics, she always says she would like to have a simpler meal planner to share. "Boys," she says, "I need a menu planner. I want it to fit inside a purse. I want it to make sense, and I want it affordable." Good luck!

To answer this request, we put one together. It is "mom-approved" and can help with your budgeting and menu planning. It is called the *Frontiersmen* Planner. This goes along with our *Frontiersmen* games we made with our family. For more information on the *Frontiersmen Series* see the additional resources section in the back of the book.

Now, if you really use meal scheduling and begin to plan and monitor where your money is going, then you will be more inclined to save. However, if you just throw your money away so you can always have what you want without effort, then you get what you get.

Guilt

Where were we? Oh yes, shopping.

When we want to buy something, even a piece of candy, our dad says, "Is that a good investment?" or "Is that something you need?" If we want to buy a toy, Dad is right there, "Is that the best use of your money?" Why can't he just let us spend our money the way we want? Now, every time we go to the store we have to think about our purchases.

We've got Mom telling us to find a way to make our grocery money stretch. And that stays with us when she is not there and then we've got our dad's words embedded in our heads. It is not like they are telling us what to do, but they are asking us to think through our choices. And their looks and words haunt us at the checkout stand.

Let us ask you a question or two. When you buy things, what do you think about? Do you just spend money because you think you need it? Or do you buy because it is a habit?

Believe us when we tell you there is a lot of stuff that isn't a need. It is not that you can't have good, fun things, it is just that you need to make sure the first purchases you make with your money are ones that can increase the amount you have.

- Some people put money in the stock market.

- Some people put money in a mutual fund.

- Some people put money in tools.

- Some people put money back into their business.

- Some people put money into private investments.

- Some people put money toward their church first.

Where do you put yours? What is the first thing you do with your money when you get it? Do you just stick it in a savings account? Have you asked your bank about any other types of accounts?

Always ask. Asking gives you leverage; additional information helps you make decisions.

Guilt: a feeling of responsibility or remorse for some offense, crime, wrong, etc., whether real or imagined.

Why do we feel guilty when we spend our money on certain things? Why do we hear our dad's voice ask us those questions? We think the reason behind the guilt is once you know the difference between right and wrong, then you personally hold yourself to that responsibility. Yes, you still have the choice of your own actions, but you are personally going to have to face the results of those choices.

What happens when you leave a hammer in the rain? It rusts. It gets ruined, weak, and eventually breaks and you can't use it. That is the same with money. Money is a tool. If you want your tools to last, then you have to take care of them. You have to take responsibility in the care for your tools. In order to do that, you have to take responsibility for your actions.

You know this guilt thing isn't as bad as it seems. A good rule of thumb is if you can't tell your mom about your choice then you probably shouldn't be doing it.

Yes, we are pretty much writing down all the things that are told to us on a consistent basis. So if you are an adult, maybe these are the words you speak or maybe they are a good reminder. If you are a kid, then you are probably saying, "I can't believe I am actually reading this." No matter who you are, these are the things that worked for us. If they worked for us then they just might work for you.

One thing we would like to have super glued to your ear is *(Please don't really super glue anything to your ear):* "We can't do it for you." So that means wherever you are in your life, there is only one person that can make you move forward in a positive direction. *That person is you!* It is never too late. Just think before acting. Ask yourself questions and learn!

Tithing

Tithing: Sometimes, tithes. The tenth part of agricultural produce or personal income set apart as an offering to God or for works of mercy

We are going to reinforce the tithe and give it a little of our own twist. Some of us don't have an income. We don't have regular jobs, yet we can still pay a tithing—a tithing of time.

We don't view a tithing as a "required" charitable tax or monetary giving. We see this as a part of life, something that should be a formed habit, like opening the door for people. It should be a way you can, without thought, help others improve their situation. It can show your thanks to God for giving you the agency to choose, for giving you life and the opportunity to learn and help others, or whatever you want to thank Him for.

With that agency to choose, you have the ability to decide which direction you want your life to go. By choosing you also understand those actions will affect those around you. You can test this out. Next time you are in a store, smile and hold the door open for someone. What was his reaction? (You may have to do this a bunch of times; we did it for like an hour.)

Our mom drove us to the local shopping mall and dropped us off in front of Barnes and Noble. Deric had a pad of paper with a yes and no column. Every person that said thank you got a check in the yes column and people who ignored us got a mark in the no column. After about thirty minutes we moved to the main doors that led to the movie theater and we repeated this process.

This is what we found out. Out of the 150 people that passed through the doors we held open, ten went to a different door and opened it for themselves. We had ninety thank yous and those were primarily older people or mothers with strollers. Kids (teenagers) usually said nothing or laughed. Some people stopped and talked to us and thanked us and asked if Barnes and Noble had hired us to hold the doors open; they thought it was a nice thing for us to do.

• • •

What about tithing and depression? Do they go together?

(We aren't doctors here, so please understand we are talking about the kind of depression that goes away on its own: situational, bad test score, grounded, no dinner, missed vacations.) If you are depressed, what do you do? Some people eat, some people do not eat, and lots of people shop.

There are many times you may feel alone or without hope or that there is no use because you can't see any outcome besides gray skies. But you know what, we all have those moments. Our family has been through a lot; we have been pretty much bankrupt—well, we have been bankrupt, business bankrupt. Were those hard times? Yes and no. They were some of the best times. We went to the park and hiked in the mountains, played Frisbee, and just spent time together as a family.

Our parents did not collapse. They showed us that because one door closed, another door opened. It was not a time to throw the shovel in. It was a time to use our brains and come up with ideas.

So our parents started a consulting business, mainly for Dad. Mom worked holding seminars. Our dad consulted for power companies and electric utilities. Our mom's seminars were about running families and finances.

Anyway, we got a chance to move around to different places. We've lived in Iowa, Texas, Colorado, Washington, and Michigan. We met many people and did many community projects. It seemed the more we did: working with others, helping in park clean-ups, cemetery clean-ups, delivering Secret Santa gift baskets, working at the local plant nursery, whatever it was made our life feel better.

We did not belong to a specific church so church-donated tithing was hard to do. However, we did it when went to a church. We gave monetarily. If we went to a local diner, we would overtip the server for good service as we were leaving.

We sometimes paid for groceries when our mom felt another mom could use the help. We did this by giving the money to the checkout person.

Our tithing game was "give without being caught." It was fun, kind of like leaving May Day flowers on doorsteps.

We helped where we could. *A small interjection: We are still developing our helper skills—especially when it comes to household chores.* What did we gain from doing these things? It was the giving of time and ourselves that helped us grow. There were things that we learned that no amount of money could buy. We felt fuller and richer.

No one can tithe unselfishly if it's demanded. If it is demanded then it isn't a true tithe. Even then, we really can't say much because only God can say what is and isn't a tithe.

When you give, are you looking for thanks or recognition? Do you tithe? If so, why? How does tithing help you make money?

Tithing helps build responsibility. If you give away your money before spending it on yourself, then you are more aware of where your money is going. It is budgeting without stress.

Our mom just told us that it is important to mention when you give to your church with a true heart then that is a great thing.

It is something you should do because you want to, not because of guilt.

Another important thing to know is a lot of people spend money because they feel empty or think that they need something. Many times if you help someone or volunteer your time, you can fill that empty space.

Debt: It takes a Boy Scout

When we first got our $1,000 in Yahoo! Finance it was a good choice on our parents' part. We didn't have cash to spend at stores and the only thing we got to do was learn about basic investing.

When we sat with our dad, he showed us profit and loss statements. Yes, that is a giant scale compared to ours but it was an interesting approach. We had to learn about spending habits, what an asset is, what a loss is, and how they affect the end result on the balance sheet.

Whatever that result, it was reported to the public and then the company's stock prices rose or fell. There are other factors that make the stocks move but this is basic; take it with a grain of salt.

By listening to this we started applying it to our own money. We wanted to be a strong company. That is when we invented our "personal store." It is a game where we started paying ourselves whenever we wanted something.

If we wanted a $.50 candy, we paid ourselves $.50 and went without the candy. If we needed a pencil, we bought a pencil from the "parent store." Pencils cost $.10. We had to then update our balance sheet and mark our purchase as an asset or liability. The pencil we put down as an asset because it helped us get our jobs done. By getting our jobs done, we got money. (Going to school was our job.)

One time we wanted to buy water balloons. They were fun. We filled them up and threw all 250 of them in a matter of thirty minutes. Then we had to clean up all the little pieces of plastic and that took *a long time.* This purchase was considered a liability. Although it gave us fun, we lost time and money; there was no return on that investment.

We could have turned it into a profit by buying thousands of balloons and charging kids $5/hour to have a water balloon fight. But we didn't, and we wouldn't (at least not today).

So what is debt? Debt is something that is owed or that you are bound to pay: a liability or obligation to pay or render something. You don't get into debt by buying items *you have the money for!*

Some people go into debt to accomplish a goal that is assumed to repay the debt once it is accomplished. Some people go into debt because they want their wants and can't wait until they save the money for them. Some people go into debt because of unforeseen events or accidents. Most people go into debt to buy their house or car.

The question is how to get out of debt. There are a lot of books and people talking about debt and getting rid of debt. The first thing you should do is budget.

We have been in and out of the Boy Scouts growing up. We have earned several merit badges. Most merit badges went along with our lifestyles—hiking, camping, swimming, first aid, environmental science, citizenship in the community, citizenship in the nation, citizenship in the world, emergency preparedness, family life, and personal management. The list goes on. Below is what the Boy Scouts do as part of their merit badge requirements.

Why don't you take a look? Why don't you try it?! We'd be interested in seeing if what you do helps.

Prepare a budget: write down all your income (allowance, jobs, and birthday money), all your expenses (purchases), and all your savings.

Then keep track of your actual income, purchases, and what you save for thirteen weeks in a row.

It's not that hard; it only takes a little effort.

Here is a record sheet you can use:

• • •

Date							
Income							
Savings							
Housing							
Food							
Car							
Auto Ins.							
Life Ins.							
Schl Loan							
Gifts							
Clothes							
Carry Over							
Balance							

• • •

Have you ever wanted to go into business for yourself? Well, we have good news! You are in business for yourself! Your job is your client: when you help your client, you get paid. Then you have to take that pay, that money, and apply it to your business financials (your budget worksheet).

Companies make investments. It is their goal to profit. That's why they are there. That is why you work too, to make money.

So now that you are a business, what kind of things do you want to tighten up? What are your spending habits? How do you feel when you buy something or pay a bill? Was that money well spent? Do you need all the bells and whistles?

We started making our money when we started running our life like a business. It is fun; it is challenging. You live one time, so you might as well find a way to smile when you work.

By setting up your "business," you have a goal that everyone in the family can work toward. It doesn't have to be strictly financial; money is just a good tool to have around.

• • •

What happens if your business is in debt already? Well, get out of it.

You need to take your credit cards and empty them. That means, don't use them and pay them off with whatever money you can! Pay them off one at a time. Once one is paid for, then move on to the next.

You need to cut expenses, reduce the amount of money going out to things like going to the movies (get Netflix). Make your own food; take your date on a picnic.

Once you battened down the hatches and have your debt paid off, then you are already used to your new lifestyle and can start investing the money you used to pay off your debt.

Okay, Mom, we'll remind them. At this time we'd like to inform you that we are not certified financial advisors and cannot advise you on *anything*. Please seek professional help when considering this or any other financial advice. Please seek your doctor's advice before starting on this or any other lifestyle change. We would also like to remind you that *"You have a brain, use it!"*

The Refrigerator Job Board

One weekend about a year ago we woke up to nothing. No mom, no dad, just a note on the stair banister saying we had no money and with no money there would be no food or place to stay. Our camping packs were packed and we were asked to leave. You have to understand our house runs strangely on a regular basis; we are thrown into situations with no clue of what to expect, like this one.

Once we were outside pitching our tent, some lady (Mom) came by announcing jobs would be posted on the fridge. They were first come, first serve.

We dropped our packs and lined up as she posted the job board. We eagerly looked at what was available and signed our names next to the jobs we would take.

Each job stated who we needed to report to and what the pay was. We could sign up for more than one; however, if we didn't get all we signed up for done, then we'd owe the amount of money for those jobs.

It stunk to be the last one signing up because all the good jobs were taken. In the afternoon a new list was posted, and we would have a different picking order based on quality of work and time taken to get the jobs done.

In some cases we had the project manager breathing down our necks (Dad) and at lunchtime there was a little diner we could go to (Café Creatous—one of Mom's diners she invented for her *Frontiersmen* game). We believe Bertha was our waitress (Mom).

After a fine meal of cracked wheat with peanut and berry squish (PB&J), we headed out to our work inspection and payroll.

This game went on for an entire weekend. It was a lot of fun and we didn't really think there was any point, but there was. It was teaching us about quality and work ethics. You see, no matter what you are doing, whether you are making your bed or writing a paper for history, you need to do your best. It's putting forth that little extra effort that doesn't cost you anything but pays off continuously.

Remember you represent your business. Are you going to produce a junk product or do you want to be known for quality?

It is easy to just throw stuff together and most of the time others won't notice or care, but you will know. Is that something you want to live with? Just floating through life without caring?

Don't get us wrong, there are plenty of times when you just shove your clothes under your bed so your room looks clean, totally understandable. But eventually you will have to put them away properly, and if they stay jammed under there long enough, then you need to rewash them and pretty much start all over.

What is the quality of your products? Are they a quality that you would like to share with others?

Remember you are an example, whether you want to be or not. There is someone who looks up to you. You can influence those around you to do their best by setting a positive example.

Pulling Weeds

With the help of our dad and mom we began a real test of our skills. For years now we have been reading financial articles, listening to our parents' talks, hanging out with our mom while she is teaching her classes, and working with our dad on power projects. We learned about world markets and how all of economies is linked. We've learned about the United States Great Depression and the hyper-inflation that happened in Germany. We've been challenged by both of our parents to come up with ideas and ways to put our skills to use.

Job One: The Power Ball

We know that leveraging can be risky. It is a good way to get into debt if what you're leveraging for doesn't work out. But we thought we'd take the risk and see what happens. So, we took a loan, a little leveraging from our parents, and bought a box of Power Balls. They are handheld tops (gyros) that accelerate to incredibly high speeds as your wrist moves in circles.

First we had to establish a marketing plan. A marketing plan is usually a written paper that says how you are going to get people to know about and buy your product. But as usual, we kind of set out on a spontaneous marketing plan. We knew what we wanted to do and made notes, but did not actually make a formal presentation. Plus, our mom was right there making "suggestions."

The first places we went were high school football games. We did this because when you get the Power Ball up to a certain speed, it acts like a generator and lights up in bright colors. So all we had to do was spin it and people came to us. At three football games we sold about twenty. We had eighty more to go.

The next area we hit was the military base gym. Our approach here was to challenge the muscle men to a Power Ball dual. David had become proficient at a stringless start. He could quickly get the rotations per minute up to a solid 10,000 and beyond. He made it look easy.

So these men, who were very nice and humored our challenge, got a chance to see how much strength it took to keep the gyro moving and many of them left our experiment stretching and massaging there forearms, hands, and wrists. We sold about five, including a military discount. So that is twenty-five down and seventy-five to go.

It was now heading into the Christmas shopping season. Thanksgiving was just around the corner. We called the shopping malls to see if we could set up a little kiosk but they wanted $3,000 a month! Forget it! We had to find a way to get people to see our product without the expense.

So we just walked the streets, parking lots, and played our toys in restaurants; we figured buying milkshakes tasted better and cost much less then $3,000 for a tile square in the mall.

Our plan worked. People asked what the Power Balls were and where we got them. We told them we sold them; we were working on our entrepreneur merit badge for scouts. Everyone was interested and we sold the remaining seventy-five. In the end we paid back our parents and enjoyed many milkshakes.

However, we learned that we aren't much for selling objects. It was fun but there is too much involved, unless we were the ones to develop the product and allow others to sell it for us. Then objects work well in our eyes.

We learned things that we would have never learned in school: budgeting, how prices are determined, what goes into marketing, and having a plan. In school we don't even really get a chance to see how algebra applies to everyday life. We sometimes learn a little about budgeting, but in reality there is no real financial education.

So how in the heck are we supposed to learn these things? Like what we really need to know to live on our own, and what options are available to us. What about following dreams?

Most people think the only choices or opportunities out there are those that are in the text books. This is a good place to say one of our family mottos: "The first person had to learn it somewhere; be the first." This means take a chance, give yourself a hypothesis, and set out to find the answer. It could take years, but at least you're engaged.

People always say they are looking for outside-of-the-box thinkers. But when you try to do that you are told to go back to the book. So which one is it?

Are people afraid to learn something new, another way things work, or something that might prove an old thought wrong? Something that is not in the book? What about you, do you just go about your day inside your box? How often do you open the window and look out?

How do you open the box? That is a good question, and the answer is simple. Don't watch too much TV, don't have your primary focus be on what the movie stars are doing. Instead, when you talk to someone, listen to him and pay attention. We have so many things around us that could be improved or invented. Some things just need to be seen from a different angle.

Many people say they want those who can forward think, but they are not ready to see or hear the ideas. The forward thinkers move on and often start their own companies. You can do this! Say your ideas aloud. Say them, try them, and learn from them. When you have an idea, write it down. The more you challenge yourself to improve or find solutions, the more your brain will develop out of the box.

. . .

Since we doubted our selling skills, we set out to find another way to make a profit. We found weeds—weeds of all sorts that nobody needs. So one day we started pulling them out. One by one, step by step, we pulled, we plucked, and we got stung and cut and cranky. We never wanted to pull weeds again. That is until people started paying us. Then we learned about service-based jobs. That is a good area to be in. The overhead is low and the return is high, as long as you are getting paid what you are worth.

We followed our mom's advice and told people to pay us on the quality. Some people paid rather low, because we are just kids. But most people paid a fair rate, because we had high standards.

Our personal business was on a roll. We gave our money to our parents; it was time to start investing. We just bought our stock through our parents' accounts and kept track of what and how much we owned. At first we checked the account every day. Or just went on to Yahoo! Finance and typed in the stock's symbol. Then we gradually moved on to checking the stock once a week, and now only when we remember.

We have seen our account reach super highs and drop back to below our purchase price and rise again. One of our stocks we bought at $2.04 reached $8.50. That is a good return in a year. But finding the right stock is more than just giving your money to a company you like. You need to research and be ready to buy when you find the company or industry that has promise.

Today, we are busy with our landscaping. We design and build garden structures (rudimentary) and do general yard maintenance. This is not what we have planned for our futures, but for right now it is going well. David has also started caring for animals while people are on vacation.

It is nice to have your own money to pay for driver's education (David's most recent purchase). Or buy things that your family can do or share (board games or cards).

It is important to know what goes on in the world of money. It is different than what most people think. It is more than paying rent and buying groceries. If it is used right it can be fun, and it can be there when you need it.

The basic things you need to do and learn are mentioned throughout this book:

- Learn to budget

- Learn to research

- Learn to listen

- Learn to invest

- Learn to save

- Learn to care

- Learn to think

- Learn to stand up for what you believe in

- Learn your value

If you do what you've learned then you not only make money, but you can add wealth.

• • •

Looking ahead, we've written a personal business plan together. This basically outlines our goals, what steps we are going to take to get there, and what our plans are if some of the circumstances change, like what we would do if our path is blocked. When we get discouraged, we can review this plan and it helps get us back on track.

Our next venture is much bigger, and we have a presentation/business plan we are going to take to Angel Investors. Now finding these investors is one thing, but getting a chance to actually present to them is another. There are many people trying to do the same thing. So we have registered with a Web site that helps link the two groups together, but again, that is still hard.

In addition to trying to get into the investors' line of sites, we have to convince them we can do the project. We believe we can do it. We believe there is a huge upside. We know that we have a great foundation and support to carry the whole thing through.

So what is the project you say?

It has to do with a research project. We have several experienced people working with us. We'll be able to tell you more when the project gets underway!

But why do we want to get involved in a project we can't tell you about? Because it is intriguing and we know we can do it. We believe in it. And we want it. In the end, the return on investment will help us gain a financial foundation for school and our futures. We have many goals and want to get going. Sometimes people need to take the next step; otherwise it is like treading water, waiting for the current to take them to shore. There are only two things that are certain while you are in the water: If you wait for the current, even if you see land, you can drown and if you're lucky you will get washed up to shore and dragged out. If you see the shore and start swimming, you can still drown or you will get stronger and reach the shore, ready to continue.

Writing a business plan opens many doors on its own. You should think of writing a business plan for your own life—your personal business. If you do, just wait to see what happens!

• • •

This book is actually part of our own personal business plan. It is an important step really. We want to see others get a chance to start on their goals. We like to hear about what other people have done to get where they are. This book is like a stepping stone, and we'll see where it leads us.

• • •

Back to our future projects, we are looking at a bigger picture. We have the time to put 100% into seeing them through, and is this taking away from our childhood? Not in our eyes. This is an awesome way to spend your child-hood. We don't watch a lot of TV (but we do get to watch the things our parents rent from Netflix–we are currently watching the King Fu television show). We don't really play video games; we spend our time outside letting our imaginations go. Planning out goals is fun. We can do it while we float down the river, we can talk about it on car trips, and we can have fun working toward these goals. We have now, however, hit a point where we want to move on; we feel like we are stagnating, just waiting to get started.

• • •

Okay, our presentation skills need a little refining. (Who are you kidding, Devin? We need a lot of refining!) In order to help with this problem our mom has encouraged us to talk to people; we usually just hang out together and plan. Of course we have taken this request of "talking to people" to heart.

Every morning after swim practice we walk to Wendy's while Deric is in the pool. David goes in and orders a frosty or something, acting normal and polite. Then Devin enters. Have you ever seen the show "Mork and Mindy"? Our parents rented this from Netflix for us. There is a character called Exidor. Devin comes in acting the mix between Exidor and Kramer from "Seinfeld" with a twist of "Mr. Bean." Every day he does something different and the workers get a good laugh. He's ordered everything from lobster and shrimp cocktail to peanut butter sandwiches. As you can see we are working hard on our communication skills.

Financial Layer 8

Emergency Preparedness

When you have saved and made a comfortable amount of money, it is time to start thinking about a rainy day. We all have them. Do not underestimate your situations because you never know what's ahead.

While we were shopping for groceries one day we thought about camping. Who thinks about camping while they shop? We'll tell you who, not many people. In fact, when we mentioned camping and finance in the same sentence we get looks like, "These kids have lost their marbles." (Just for your own information, our marbles are safely stored in the toy closet next to our jacks and cards.)

This is how our brains connected camping and grocery stores. When camping, you are totally self-reliant. You either have food, find food, or starve. When you go to the store, you are totally dependent. How many people take for granted that they can just run in and buy a loaf of bread anytime they need it?

Yes, it is convenient, that is the whole point. But you have someone else doing the work for you. How many of you know how to make bread? How many have actually done it? Okay, since you all have, just go with us on this for a moment.

If you went to the store and bought all the ingredients to make a loaf of bread, it would cost you *a lot* more than just picking one up. But, what if you bought enough to make fifty-two loaves (one for each week of the year)? Then you are getting closer to the store price. Yes, you still have to count for your time, but it usually pays off in taste.

Now you are saying, What is the benefit of having a year's worth of bread?

Okay, here is our money-saving and emergency food plan. What if your garage was stocked like a grocery store (less the fresh fruits and veggies)? You would save money in gas, you would save money on stocking fees, you would save money on time to go to the store, and price per pound is cheaper.

But how much cheaper is your garage grocery store, and would the taste/quality be the same? By having the grocery garage you could save up to 75% of your normal grocery bill. And the quality and taste (if you buy right) is good!

How do we know this? Remember when we said we were told to do the shopping for our family? Well we did. We now have a grocery store garage! And it is great! It takes a few minutes to cook our foods from scratch or semi-scratch and the flavor isn't bad. In fact, we all eat it!

We spent $4,800 for the year in bulk. We have everything from sourdough bread to chili, to drink mixes, veggies, fruits, pasta, desserts, sauces, and much more! We now budget about $200 a month for fresh stuff and personal items/cleaning supplies.

We are hungry boys and eat a lot in our home.

Our food does more than just save us money. It is also good for emergencies. You always hear of people running to the stores before a storm comes in. The shelves are emptied from their water supplies and other things.

Well, guess what? When a storm hits we don't need to make that run and we are learning how to depend on ourselves in a sense. You see, for any emergency preparedness the only thing you have to count on is yourself. If you are resourceful, you will find a way to make a shelter, block the sun, drink the water, and eat. Your financial emergency is the same; you are responsible for seeing that you have all you need.

The more you actually do, like the example of making bread from scratch, the more you learn and then you have more confidence in your actions. The more you know how to do and the more you are willing to do it, can also end up encouraging others to follow in your footsteps.

Back to the thought of self-reliance: the more you are in control of your personal business budget, the more you are prepared for a financial emergency. Try looking at it this way: if you just go to the store and pick up a loaf of bread without thinking about it because it's the easiest, *you are* making yourself *dependent on everyone else* involved in making the bread for you. And many of you don't even know what's in it.

Is that how you want to live? Without knowing what's in it? That can definitely be more comfortable, we agree.

And most of the time we just trust that our parents will do it all and we don't have to think about it.

But what really stinks are the pop quizzes that hit just when we don't think we have to think. Like when our parents say out of the blue, "What would you have done in this situation? Why? What would the chain reaction be to that choice?"

We are going to give you a situation and then we want you to ask yourself the questions above.

Once upon a time there was a rabbit. It was so cute and fluffy and needed a home.

You have a huge dog at home that loves to chase and catch birds. You really want the bunny and think you could find a way to keep it in your backyard (your dog lives out there too). You also have a friend that keeps rabbits.

What would happen if you brought the rabbit home? What would happen if you kept it with your dog? What would happen if you gave it to your friend that already has rabbits?

And no, you may not eat the rabbit. (Well, okay only if you are totally starving and didn't have a good food storage system. We are trying to keep this book at a "G" rating and seeing how upset people are about Bambi, we should probably change our story.)

Story rewrite:

You are a lifeguard at your local pool. You have been on the stand for what seems like days and weeks with nothing going on. Everyone knows the rules and very seldom do you have to tell people to walk.

On this day, you feel it is going just like all the others. Your brain wanders in thought about what you did the night before and your plans for later that night.

A few kids swim over to the deep end and hang on the wall talking. A few other kids are in the deep end diving off the wall over the kids in the water. They are all friends and having a good time.

Something makes you uneasy about the situation but they'd been doing this every afternoon throughout the summer, and so far no one has gotten hurt.

(Although this isn't making a loaf of bread it is still taking responsibility; only this shows how our choices can affect others as well.)

You might be thinking this is a made up story, but this is real. And before we tell you the result we want you to make a choice.

Do you follow your uneasy feeling and stop the kids from jumping/diving over the other kids, or do you let it go?

If you choose to stop the situation you made a good choice because you just saved a child from being paralyzed for the rest of his life. Because by letting it go, one of the kids on the wall decides to swim back to the shallow end just as one of the kids on the deck decides to jump. The jumper landed smack in the middle of the swimmer's back, and the swimmer, face down in the water, can't roll over or even lift his head to get a breath. Luckily you were able to get to him right away so he could stay alive.

Not quite as nice as the little bunny, but we bet you're paying attention now. Now we can give you the pop quiz. In every situation around you, you can ask these questions: What would you have done in this situation? Why? What would the chain reaction be to that choice?

Preparing for an emergency combines all aspects of your life. You need to be self-reliant, you need to be able to work with and help others, and you need to be prepared.

Believe in Yourself!

Who stands up for what you believe in? Who will take a chance in you? Who can find a way to keep your hope alive?

We hope you answered these questions with *you!*

Do you know how to talk, at least communicate, with others? Holy cow, that is amazing! You accomplished a goal without even knowing it!

Yes, even babies set goals, and they do a great job succeeding because they don't give themselves limitations. They just want to do the best they can.

Could you imagine if a baby fell after his first step and then just quit because it was too hard or took too much effort to balance?

You are probably thinking that is a stupid question; the baby just gets right back up and keeps going, taking breaks to eat and rest. And then once he finishes a goal he leads into the next, then the next, and then the next.

But when do we stop being that motivated, self-believing person? When are the giant boundaries of doubt built?

You are that same person, the person who wants to succeed, but maybe some of you have shrugged your shoulders and just said, "What's the use?"

We'll tell you what, you are the use! Every single person on the face of this planet has use, has ability, and has potential.

In this chapter, like the rest, we've consulted our parents. Anyway, this chapter we have used Mom to help us, due to the fact we are still kids and are learning the importance of self-worth.

We will let you know what we understand and the examples that were shown to us. But from what we know, most of the time you don't have to think about or make sure you are aware of how you think about yourself. You are who you are. But there are times when you might feel really low.

The other day we had an electrician over and we had to pull the fridge away from the wall. There was some syrup spilled with lint and cereal stuck to it, so Mom put water on it to soak.

Before we go on, let's travel back in time two weeks earlier when we were vacuuming the car. We have three vacuums: a shop-vac; a normal-looking, stand-up one; and a Simplicity canister (Mom's favorite). Now the day before, we helped Dad clean up some junk in the garage with the shop-vac. This stuff was gooey (cola syrup) and sandy and didn't dry well so it stuck all over the hose. While Mom was vacuuming the car out, this stuff kept marking the carpet. Needless to say, she tried the second vacuum only to find the electrical cord was accidentally chewed upon by something small and fluffy. So we are now down to the Simplicity vacuum, which always works for her.

Fast forward to the kitchen scene.

Wanting to surprise Mom, one of us cleaned under the fridge and used the Simplicity to suck up the syrup liquid goop, which then went into the bag after sticking along the walls of the hoses. Of course, once this junk was in the bag it leaked into the rest of the area, including the filter.

Mom walked into the kitchen and noticed right away the floor had been cleaned. She was so happy, or so we thought. When she went to the vacuum, she noticed a strange substance leaking from it. The anger built over the next several seconds; frustration hit as she looked down the hoses and then she asked in a strong voice, "Who used the vacuum to clean the stuff that was under the fridge?"

No one answered. So she asked again. The cleaner raised his hand. And some famous words flew into the air, "You have got to use your brain! Have I ever asked you or have you ever seen me suck up liquid with this vacuum? What were you thinking?!"

Now no words needed to be said. The guilty party quietly got up and left the room while Mom cleaned up the mess. About two minutes later, Mom got a look of shock on her face and went to find the "helper."

She said she was sorry for getting upset. She said that no vacuum was worth more than one of her children. She said she felt terrible (remember she didn't yell or anything). But the "helper" and Mom ended up feeling the same; their self-worth dropped to the size of a microbe.

The "helper" was just trying to do something nice; he felt really good about it and stayed around to see the results. The result crushed the positive intention. Sometimes we need to step back and take into account what is going on around us before we jump to conclusions; many times we jump without thinking.

Mom and the helper were able to recover because they both trusted in their own actions for the future; they learned and shook off the bad/sad feelings. But if they did not believe in themselves, then that bad/sad feeling would have stuck around and influenced their future.

• • •

"Believing in yourself dictates what you will do—it is the difference between doing something and doing nothing."
A quote from our dad

We are not talking about being greedy, egotistical, self-centered brats; there may be a book already made for that category. You should be confident enough to help others without looking for praise. You should voluntarily pick up the trash at the park, schoolyard, or backyard. You should gain happiness in seeing the happiness of others. And this is possible.

At winter holiday time when gifts are exchanged, do you get more excited about giving or receiving? Would you be mad if you did not get the newest electronic devices or if someone forgot your gift?

When you have the strength to stand up for what you believe in (this does not mean you have to be pushy and voice your opinion loudly; it just means you have the personal strength to live up to your own standards no matter what others around you are doing) then you are a leader. Boy, it is hard to talk about this subject because this is up to you. You have to learn that even if you can only offer to do the dishes for a friend's mom then you've done what you could and that's important. Your actions are important. And if you show that you care or believe in someone else, you bring yourself up without even knowing it.

Go ahead and take a look inside yourself and write down things you do well and ways you can help others:

Now write down ten goals worth working for. Start small on your first one and gradually build to larger goals.

Okay, now write down ten standards you want to live up to. Ten things you want to follow the rest of your life, (not doing drugs, not leaving your things all over the yard ...)

1. _____

2. _____

3. _____

4. _____

5. _____

6. _____

7. _____

8. _____

9. _____

10. _____

Well now that you have some goals and standards to live up to, when are you going to start implementing them?

We've noticed there are a bunch of books and people talking about how to start working toward your goals.

We have some really good news for you. We've found a shortcut to those questions and how to start.

This is what you should do. *Put this book down, stand up, and start living your life the way you have chosen, no matter what anyone else says or thinks.*

Oh, this is the hard part? Stand up and make that change (with a "little tiny" bit of effort on your part).

You are right, implementing changes, even small ones, is hard. But you have to believe in yourself in order to even begin. *No one* can do it for you. (See, our parents *are* right when they say that.)

• • •

So here we are, trying to conclude our book on believing in yourself, but we feel there is something missing.

If you have any ideas or stories you want to add to this let us know. Like our mom says, "We all have something to share and we all have something to gain from each other."

Afterthoughts

We went out into the world and asked people what they learned from their parents, what advice they got that proved to be true, and what advice they wish they had listened to. We also asked people what they thought the most important financial advice is that they could give.

We encourage you to take a few minutes to read through and maybe add some as you go.

And one more thing, thanks for taking time to read this book. We had fun writing it and we hope you got what you wanted out of it.

Your Own Advice

"Be independent."

Vanessa in Washington

"Stay away from credit cards."

Brad in Washington

"Wear clean underwear and keep a quarter in your pocket."

Bill in Oregon

"Be patient and take your time when you can. Otherwise, hold on for the ride."

Jenny in New York

"Save up for what you want and put your needs first."
Jake in Idaho

"Never stop learning."
Amber in Washington

"Clean your room."
Stephanie in Washington

"Don't leave your kids in the car."
Derek in Washington

"If you don't have anything nice to say then keep your mouth shut."
Brittany in Washington

"Brush your teeth before you are tired, that way you won't forget."
Jack in California

"Always be aware of your surroundings."
Molly in Oregon

"Make up your own mind."
Dianna in San Diego

"Don't follow someone too closely and go slow in the snow and ice."
Ted in Washington

"Always forgive–you just don't have to forget."
Stacey in Washington

"Listen to classical music."
Peter in Iowa

"Hold hands."
Ruth in Texas

"Learn to read a map."
Ryan in Colorado

"If you love someone, let them know."
Rachel in North Carolina

Additional Resources

Several times throughout this book we've mentioned games and tools we use at home. We call them the *Frontiersmen Series*. Within this series we have five items in print and would like to share them with you.

The first is called *Frontiersmen had no TV*. This is our family night diner that we do once a week. Our mom, who wanted to spice up dinner without complaints, originally made it. She tells her friends it also helps tame the picky eater. When we have guests over, we usually take them to the Frontiersmen Diner. It is a lot of fun. We have over twenty menus; each menu includes a brief description of the "restaurant" you are visiting.

The next is *Famivlee-a*. This game is trivia with a twist; it is based on your family history or the history of the group you are with. This is a great conversation starter and memory grabber!

Like *Famivlee-a*, *Picture-ary* grabs hold of your memory and renews conversation. This game uses your family photos.

The *Frontiersmen Planner* is a menu planner and organizer.

Finally, we have the *Frontiersmen Bank Book*. This planner includes space for your activities and helps you monitor your spending and saving activities. We use this book personally.